P9-BHR-944

FLOWERS

OVER 200 WAYS TO USE FLOWERS IN YOUR HOME

Quadrille

FLOWERS

Stephen Woodhams with Hilary Mandleberg

PHOTOGRAPHY BY LORRY EASON

First published in 2004 by
Quadrille Publishing Limited
Alhambra House, 27-31 Charing Cross Road, London WC2H OLS

This edition published by Silverback Books, Inc., San Francisco, CA.
www.silverbackbooks.com

Copyright © Text, Design and Layout 2004 Quadrille Publishing Limited

The right of Stephen Woodhams to be identified as the author of this
work has been asserted by him in accordance with the Copyright, Design
and Patents Act 1988.

Creative Director Helen Lewis
Editorial Director Jane O'Shea
Art Editor Chalkley Calderwood Pratt
Text Hilary Mandleberg
Production Beverley Richardson

All rights reserved. No part of this book may be reproduced, stored in
a retrieval system, or transmitted in any form or by any means, electronic,
electrostatic, magnetic tape, mechanical, photocopying, recording or
otherwise, without prior permission, in writing, of the publisher.

Based on material originally published in Flower Power.

British Library Cataloguing-in-Publication Data
A catalogue record for this book is available from the British Library.

ISBN 1-59637-009-2

Printed in China

Contents

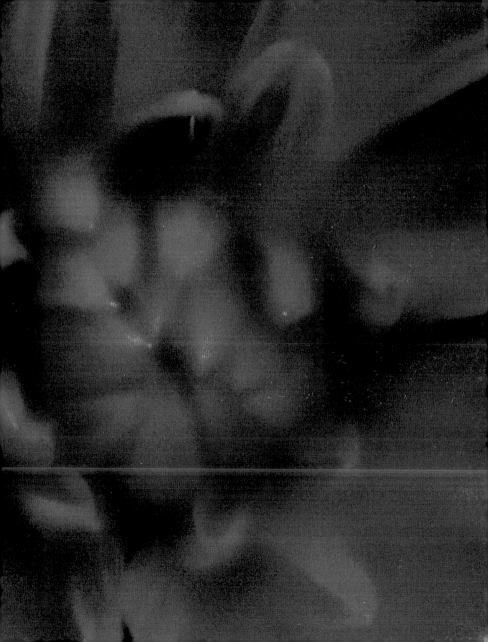

VUYLSTEKEARA CAMBRIA ORCHID

Orchids are among the sexiest of all flowers, and the tropical-looking, rich red-and-white Vuylstekeara Cambria orchid is one of the best that nature has to offer.

■ Its exotic, complex flowers can be as big as 3 inches across. Just one on its own in a simple vase will pack a punch.
■ This orchid adds a dose of magically intense color, especially in a richly decorated, dark-paneled room.

GERBERA

Gerberas are always on my shopping list. I love their strong, open, honest simplicity. This pink one boasts a ruff of smaller petals around its center.

■ Try just a single gerbera bloom in a matching pink bud vase. It will last at least a week.

■ Put some purple gravel in the bottom of a goldfish bowl, half-fill with water, and float a few pink gerbera heads on top. Magic!

HELICONIA

Unsurprisingly, one of the common names for this spiky, abstract-looking plant is "lobster claw." The dramatic red triangles you see aren't flowers but bracts, or modified leaves.

■ Heliconia's strongly graphic look makes it the perfect choice for a minimalist arrangement in a contemporary room.
■ The leaves are large and resemble those of the banana palm. Here they've been removed to show the red bracts in all their glory.

BELLADONNA LILY

The scent of the belladonna lily
is one of my favorites. It is a native
of South Africa, where it flowers
before its leaves appear, which
is why one of its common names
is "naked ladies."

■ It is found mostly in this
stunning, clear pink, but is also
beautiful in white.

■ In the garden, it does best
against a south-facing wall or in
deep pots on a sunny porch.

FLOWERING CABBAGE

Flowering cabbages are superb for winter color. This pink variety is a beauty. They also come in green and purple, but I like the white ones best.

■ If you don't have a proper garden, they also look great planted in pots on a patio or in a windowbox. Try purple ones in a galvanized container.

■ Flowering cabbages can make a dinner-party centerpiece that doesn't get in the way of the conversation.

TULIP

The world of red tulips is vast, ranging from the plainest single ones through fringed and doubles to mind-blowing parrot tulips.

■ A hand-tied bunch of red tulips with a collar of Swiss cheese plant leaves makes a fabulous Valentine's Day gift.

■ Try filling a black or brown cube-shaped vase with wet florist's foam and arranging red tulip heads in it in a grid pattern. It would look great on a coffee table.

PHOTINIA 'RED ROBIN'

This excellent garden shrub has new spring leaves that are a beautiful bronze-red. To encourage this spectacular foliage, you need to cut it back quite hard after the foliage has faded to dull bronze.

■ Try Photinia 'Red Robin' in any arrangement with other reds and purples. It will look stunningly opulent.
■ The mature leaves turn a rich green. Their strong shape makes them also useful as a base foliage.

"ICED TEA" ROSE

This miniature rose with a light scent and slightly faded-looking russet blooms was first bred in the United States. Commercially grown roses all have evenly matched heads and stems, which makes them easier to use for flower arranging.

■ Try it in a traditional rose nosegay, punctuated with lime green lady's mantle and edged with lady's mantle leaves.
■ It also works well for contrast when used in mixed cottage-garden arrangements in pinks and lilacs.

FLOWERING CHERRY

This delicate harbinger of spring originated in Japan and is often portrayed in old Japanese prints and drawings. It is related to plum and almond trees.

■ Put a few stems in a simple, oriental-style vase and revel in their calm, Zen-like quality.

■ Try lining a glass vase with any large green leaves, adding wet florist's foam, then arranging some cherry blossom stems in the center with a collar of light pink roses.

DOGWOOD

Some shrubby forms of dogwood are useful in winter, with bare stems that range from red to green, adding a welcome splash of color. They have many uses for flower arrangers.

■ Try red dogwood stems at Christmas, mixed with other winter foliage and wrapped around containers, or for staking amaryllis.

■ Young greenish-yellow dogwood stems work well wrapped around the stems of dried-flower trees.

RANUNCULUS

The soft, rounded flowers of ranunculus are so perfect you might almost think they were made from tissue paper. Besides this deep pink, they come in a multitude of other colors—white, yellows, reds, and oranges—all fading gracefully as they age.

■ Ranunculus work well without any other flowers or foliage in single or mixed-color arrangements.
■ Buy one as a plant, and put it in a color-matched flowerpot.

Get the look
with reds

Reds encompass bold, dramatic true
red as well as soft pink. Some reds
are so dark they are almost black.
Use strong red on its own, especially
in arrangements of one variety of
flower, for a look that's contemporary,
but soften it with contrasting foliage,
and it gets to be more classic.

PEONY PERFECT

Peonies are normally thought of as traditional cottage-garden flowers, but they don't have to be. Here I've given them a modern look by arranging them in a contemporary blue wire mesh container and letting the blooms speak for themselves.

1

Fill the vase with soaked florist's foam (page 300).

2

Use an odd number of Japanese-style pink peonies.

3

Arrange them so their heads appear just over the edge of the container.

4

Complete by adding darker pink semi-double blooms to the top to give a gently rounded effect.

DUTCH STILL LIFE

This traditional arrangement of double and Japanese-style peonies reminds me of a Dutch still life painting. It makes the most of the peony's wonderful color range and characteristic "over the top" blooms. It would suit a country interior to perfection.

1
Line an old terracotta flowerpot with plastic sheeting and fill with soaked florist's foam (page 300).

2
Place the tallest peony stems in the center and arrange the shorter ones around to make a tall cone shape.

3
Finish with a few long-stemmed peonies around the edge of the pot and some trailing stems of jasmine.

RED NERINE

Put this tiny arrangement on a desk and it would give anyone the urge to get on with their work. It shows how a single flower stem can be as effective as a whole bunch.

1
Choose a vase in a bold colour and with a simple shape, like this terrific little orange vase.

2
Simply add water and one beautiful stem of nerine in a harmonising colour.

■ TIP:
An allium head or a single orchid would work well too.

RED EXUBERANCE

In this arrangement, the exuberance of the arching stems of scarlet plume and of the 'James Storey' orchids is given free rein. It just needs the chunky container to ground the composition.

1
Make a moss collar (page 300), fix it around a shallow plastic bowl, then cover with wired bunches of box foliage.

2
Fill the bowl with crumpled chicken wire and half fill with water.

3
Use Skimmia japonica 'Rubella' for a base, followed by the scarlet plume and stems of 'James Storey' orchids.

4
Thread through clusters of deep red 'Black Magic' roses.

STAIRWAY TO HEAVEN

Industrial-style containers capture the pared-down style of contemporary interiors. Here I have teamed glass test tubes with flowering pink cabbages and have hung them from a traditional wooden banister rail for a striking contrast. The test tubes highlight the chunky stems of the cabbages.

1
Twist together two long strands of fine wire, then wrap them several times around the lip of a test tube.

2
Loop the long ends of wire around a banister rail and twist together securely to fasten. Repeat twice more.

3
Fill each test tube two-thirds full with water.

4
Insert a stem of flowering cabbage in each tube, removing the lower leaves so the cabbage head sits perfectly.

■ TIP:

A drop of household bleach plus regular changes of water, stops the water from smelling.

BELLADONNA BEAUTY

I find the pure, old-fashioned quality of the belladonna lily completely irresistible, whether used as part of a mixed arrangement or on their own, as here. "Bella donna" means "beautiful lady." How true!

1
Fill a clear glass vase two-thirds full with water.

2
Make a base of the mauveish-purple foliage of Rosa glauca syn. R. rubrifolia.

3
Weave in stems of belladonna lily—they have several flowers to a stem—so they rise above the foliage.

THE HEAT IS ON

Some color contrasts really shock with their audacity, and this arrangement is a great example. You may think you're looking at a harmonious mix of colors, but in fact you're seeing dramatic contrasts in color temperature—hot burgundy, yellow, and orange alongside cool purple.

1
Fill a rectangular galvanized container with some crumpled chicken wire and half-fill with water.

2
Trim the stems of the tulips so their heads sit just above the edge of the container.

3
Arrange the tulips in blocks of color.

BOTTLED UP

I remember tulips well from my student days at the Royal Horticultural Society Gardens at Wisley, in Surrey, so I have a special fondness for them. I especially love these double ones. They need no adornment at all.

1
Half-fill three identical clear glass bottles. I used milk bottles here.

2
Trim the stems of three double tulips, and pop one in each milk bottle.

3
Line the bottles up on a kitchen windowsill or narrow table.

THE SIREN'S CALL

Tulips continue to grow after they have been cut, so their stems curve and twist and their petals open wide, displaying contrasting stamens and often a contrasting throat, too. I think they look like sirens luring sailors to their death.

1
Choose a flattish clear glass vase and almost fill it with water.

2
Cut the tulips to roughly the same length. Just a few will do.

3
Pop them in the vase and leave them to do their own thing.

TULIPOMANIA

When you see parrot tulips, with
their amazing feathered and twisted
petals, you may not be surprised to
know that fortunes were won and
lost over tulip bulbs during Holland's
seventeenth-century "tulipomania."
I've even heard parrot tulips
described as "sex on legs." This one
is 'Estella Rijnveld'. She is famous
for having more "feathers" than
most. I think she looks as delicious as
a bowl of raspberry ripple ice cream.

You can't beat a mass of parrot tulips, but sometimes it's fun to add something unexpected, like these Magnolia grandiflora leaves. They not only contrast with the tulips but have their own textural contrast—a soft suede-effect underside and a glossy top surface.

1
Half-fill a square-section, V-shaped clear glass vase with water.

2
Tie the tulip stems into a tight nosegay about halfway down, then trim them all to the same length.

3
Arrange the magnolia leaves around the tulips, tying them tightly with raffia as you go.

4
Trim the ends of the raffia and pop the whole bouquet in the vase.

SINUOUS SHAPES

The clean lines of this metal-framed test-tube holder and the clarity of its glass tubes make a marvelous container for single-stem specimens such as these wonderful pink calla lilies. Arranged in this way, the individual beauty of each flower becomes part of a strong whole.

No wonder calla lilies are florists' favorites and have been for many years. Just look at the gradation of color in this pink specimen, from the almost burgundy tips of its petals to its pale pink-veined center.

■ TIP:
Four orchid heads would look magnificent too.

1
Cut four calla lilies so their heads just sit on top of the test-tube holder.

2
Line them up in the water-filled holder. Stand back and enjoy!

POT THE RED

Red is such a strong color that it often needs nothing more than the green of some foliage to set it off. This arrangement would look stunning placed on a side table under a lamp to bring out the richness of its colors.

1
Line a terra-cotta flowerpot with plastic sheeting and fill with soaked florist's foam (page 300).

2
Make a base of berried ivy and cotoneaster.

3
Weave in some ornamental crabapple, red nerines, hypericum, 'Tamango' spray roses and 'Vicky Brown' roses.

4
Finish with spiky Pavonia x gledhillii pods and burgundy snapdragons, and some pokeweed to soften the edge of the pot.

GLADIOLUS LINEUP

Laid along a shallow dish, single gladiolus flowers can make a very quick and simple table centerpiece. The longer the table and the dish, the more powerful the effect will be.

1
Cut the tips of some gladiolus stems to give pieces with at least two open flowers and some buds.

2
Position the dish on the table, and line up the cut pieces in it.

3
Pour in water, taking care not to overfill the dish.

■ TIP:
You could float the heads in a shallow glass bowl of water, instead.

ARCHITECTURAL ASPIRATIONS

Gladioluses are architectural flowers, and I hope this arrangement in a concrete block installation on the floor reflects that. It would be a real focal point—and talking point—in a large, minimal space.

1
Set a tall, square metal vase in one cavity of a concrete block, and quarter-fill the vase with water.

2
Add the tallest stems of red gladiolus you can find, including plenty of foliage to set off their red color.

3
Fill the other cavity of the concrete block with a plastic container so it can't be seen.

4
Fill the plastic container with a pair of big, rolled-up Farfugium japonicum leaves.

VENETIAN SPLENDOR

The great thing about gladiolus is that it can make a neat link between modern and traditional. This arrangement of gladioluses in a contemporary vase of blown glass and metal, standing in front of an ornate Venetian glass mirror proves the point.

1
All you need is six tall stems of gladiolus and a very tall vase. Half-fill the vase with water.

2
Arrange three tall stems in the vase, followed by three shorter ones.

A BASKET OF SWEET PEAS

This broom-wrapped basket of sweet peas and lady's mantle is a heady reminder of summer. If you were making it as a centerpiece for a summer party, you could use the leftover pieces of broom to tie up the napkins for your guests.

1
Make a moss collar (page 300), fix it around a shallow plastic bowl, then cover with wired bunches of broom.

2
Fill the bowl with crumpled chicken wire and half-fill with water.

3
Make a base of large clusters of lady's mantle.

4
Add clusters of sweet peas in shades of pink, cascading around the edges and added to the top for height.

■ TIP:
A couple of stems
of bright red
orchids would
pack a punch, too.

RED-HOT CHILI PEPPERS

This arrangement only goes to show how easy it is to make something out of nothing. It is sure to be a talking point. The silver can, with its touch of red lettering, highlights the raw sexiness of the sprig of shiny red chili peppers.

1
Remove the lid from an old drink can, tie a piece of string around the rim, making a loop from the ends.

2
Attach the loop to a hook on the wall, and add water.

3
Pop a nice bushy sprig of chili peppers in the can, stand back, and be amazed!

FLOATING GERBERAS

If you have just brought some gerberas home and a few stems have gotten damaged, there is no need to discard them. Try this ever-so-simple but effective idea. I've used deep red 'Chateau' gerberas. Don't you just love the contrasting yellow stamens?

1
Choose a bowl to complement the color of the gerberas. Silver shows off the deep red of the flowers.

2
Fill with water, cut the stems off the gerberas, and just float them in the water.

3
Put the bowl on a coffee or dining table, and admire the view.

SUMMER SIZZLER

The great thing about gerberas is
that you don't need many to pack
a punch—and they last for ages.
Arrange them in a bright array of
colored plastic glasses and they
look almost plastic themselves.

1
Choose plastic
glasses in a
color to
contrast with
the gerberas.
These bright
yellow ones do
the trick nicely.

2
Add water and
one gerbera
head to each,
trimmed so
it sits neatly
on the rim of
the glass.

3
Arrange the
glasses as
you please.

HOT STUFF

This striking arrangement has interesting things going on at three different levels. At the top are the bold red heliconia, in the middle is the collar of flat green Farfugium japonicum leaves, and beneath that the vase is stuffed full of ornamental red peppers. It's getting hot in here.

I love putting flowers, fruits and other ingredients behind glass or Perspex plastic. It adds another dimension, magnifying and high-lighting their color. Here you can see how the stems of the ornamental red peppers are enlarged and their color beautifully enhanced.

1
Three-quarters-fill a tall cylin-drical glass vase with water and pack with whole stems of ornamental red peppers.

2
Add two tall stems of red heliconia.

3
Finish with a flat collar of Farfugium japonicum leaves around the neck of the vase.

CLASSIC UPDATE

If it's opulence you're after, this is the arrangement for you, but its edgy feel belies its classic looks. The rusty urn sets the tone and dictates the sizzling colors that make it special. This classic yet modern combination would add pizzazz to a mantelpiece or side table in any traditional setting.

The dusky purple foliage of the well-named smoke tree, a mass of toning roses of similar flower sizes, and clusters of orange-tinged whitebeam berries for a slight autumnal flavor combine to make this arrangement very full-on.

1
Line the urn with plastic sheeting, and secure its edges with florist's tape.

2
Fill the urn with soaked florist's foam (page 300) so the foam stands roughly 4 inches above the edge.

3
Make a base of smoke tree foliage and whitebeam berries.

4
Add clusters of 'Leonardis' and 'Pareo' roses and some Rosa glauca syn. R. rubrifolia to break up the outline.

TRUE ROMANCE

This mixed arrangement in a smart, trumpet-shaped frosted glass vase is my idea of "shabby chic"— flowers with a slightly shabby coloration in a chic location. Even though the arrangement is made from fresh flowers, it reminds me of old, gently faded botanical prints.

1
Crumple some chicken wire into a ball to fit the mouth of the vase, and attach it with florist's tape.

2
Make a base of eucalyptus and Rosa glauca syn. R. rubrifolia, and add clusters of stocks followed by 'Sterling Silver' roses.

3
Weave in flag irises and 'Iced Tea' roses.

4
Add height with more Rosa glauca, and finish with more eucalyptus trailing over the edge of the vase.

I LOVE YOU

No matter what the occasion—a special celebration, a thank you, or simply a romantic gesture—a bunch of roses always makes a welcome present. This bouquet uses 'Black Magic' roses of a stunning, velvety dark red.

1
Holding five stems of berried ivy in one hand, arrange them into a bouquet.

2
Thread twelve long-stemmed roses through; make sure to give the bouquet a slightly rounded shape.

3
Tie the stems together high up using raffia, then trim to the same length.

4
Wrap with white tissue paper followed by clear cellophane. Finish with a raffia bow.

'TÊTE-À-TÊTE' NARCISSUS

With its not-too-large blooms and long flowering period, this is one of the most commonly grown miniature narcissi. It is also a very early one to flower.

■ Plant a mass of them in a glass container lined with gravel and topped with lush green bun moss.
■ If you are cutting them to bring indoors, choose them while they are still in bud, with just a bit of the yellow showing.

FOXTAIL LILIES

These versatile flowers can look traditional in mixed arrangements or strikingly modern on their own or with a few big leaves.

■ Try a dome-shaped bunch of orange gerberas, a few stems of foxtail lilies, and a collar of aspidistra leaves, all in a harmonizing vase.

■ Alternatively, line a cylindrical glass vase with green pebbles, add wet florist's foam, and fill with a fan of foxtail lilies and a handful of stems of Indian grass.

SUNFLOWER

Sunflowers mean summer. No matter where I am, if I see a field of sunflowers, it always reminds me of Italy.

■ Tie the stems of a bunch of sunflowers in two or three places with raffia to form a "tree," then arrange in a tall vase with their stems at an angle.
■ A row of saucer-shaped dishes on a rectangular table, each holding a sunflower head, is simple but stylish.

CATKINS

Catkins can be short and stubby
or long and dangling. Either way
they add a hint of spring and a
sense of movement and airiness
to an arrangement.

■ Catkins lend themselves naturally
to arrangements of spring flowers—
narcissi, tulips, hyacinths; you choose
■ You can also try them as a pretty
cascading collar to soften an
arrangement of tall, stately gladioluses.

ROSE

Roses are one of the oldest cultivated flowers. In Roman times they stood for intrigue and celebration. It is said that the emperor Nero's extravagance with roses was one of the causes of the collapse of the Roman Empire!

■ These striking 'Pareo' roses look stunning with flowers of a similar "temperature," such as warm yellows, reds, and purples.

■ Try them mixed with autumnal-colored foliage—dark burgundy-red cordyline, for instance.

PAPHIOPEDILUM ORCHID

This lovely Paphiopedilum 'Maudiae' is my favorite. Its flower reminds me of a bumble bee—the very insect it is designed to attract for pollination.

■ A single stem of paphiopedilum in a clear glass bowl will make a bold statement in a contemporary room.
■ Put a pot of Paphiopedilum 'Maudiae' in a glass vase lined with purple sand and top with some more of the sand to complement the hint of purple in the flower.

GERBERA

Gerberas are very versatile. I usually use them as cut flowers, but a mixture of colors planted in an old wooden trug looks quite funky.

■ Yellow gerberas look great mixed with orange ones in a dome-shaped hand-tied bunch arranged in a glass cube lined with orange and lemon slices.

■ Get a simple, fresh new look with a row of glass test tubes stuck to a window, each tube filled with a yellow gerbera.

VARIEGATED PITTOSPORUM

Pittosporums are great garden shrubs, but as they are slow-growing, you are unlikely to want to cut them. Commercially grown large- or small-leafed variegated varieties are available to buy, instead.

■ Pittosporum leaves go with most color palettes, and their variegation will add sparkle to any arrangement.
■ Try them with white tulips for a fabulous hand-tied bouquet.

RUDBECKIA

These flowers brighten the garden in late summer and early fall.
As with most open-faced flowers, positioning them at different angles in an arrangement shows off their shape to best advantage.

■ The rudbeckia is useful for "punctuating" any arrangement of autumnal flowers and foliage.

■ If you want to grow it outdoors, try planting it in chrome or glass containers for the patio or window box.

Get the look with yellows

I love using yellow, from pale lemon yellow hyacinths to egg-yolk yellow sunflowers. It's a color that always lifts the spirits. Cool it down with touches of blue, or warm it up with zingy orange. Accompanied by nothing more than their foliage, yellow flowers are sunny and lively.

TRAPPED TULIPS

Tulips never fail to please me.
Whether you indulge in huge
bunches or yearn for the simplicity
of a single specimen, there truly
are tulips for every style and mood.
Here I've taken the idea of a
vase full of tulips to the extreme.

■ TIP:
A row of tulip-filled
vases lined up on
a long table looks
super-stunning.

1
Quarter-fill a
clear glass tank
vase with water.

2
Arrange a mass
of yellow tulips
in your hand,
tying them with
raffia low down
the stems.

3
Trim the
stems to the
same length
and stand them
in the vase.

NARCISSI GALORE

This vase is one of my favorites. Its metal frame, holding clear glass test tubes, can be bent to the shape you want. Here I've made it into a circle for a centerpiece on a round table. See it again on pages 272–3.

1
Fill all the tubes of the vase with water to the same level.

2
Trim some stems of 'Paper White' and 'Soleil d'Or' narcissi to the same length.

3
Arrange in the test tubes, alternating clusters of the two different narcissi.

A BURST OF SUNSHINE

This arrangement almost looks as if it is floating on air. The clear, chunky glass vase magnifies the stems of the narcissi in an interesting way. I packed in as many stems as I could to produce a substantial, compact head of flowers.

1
Half-fill the vase with water and trim a mass of narcissi so they are about twice as tall as the vase.

2
Arrange them in the vase so they fan out very slightly.

3
Finish by adding shorter narcissi around the edge.

FRESH FROM THE GARDEN

These white Christmas roses and forsythia look as if they have just been picked from the garden. Christmas roses are truly wonderful, with their nodding heads on long, elegant stems. In addition to white, they come in pink, burgundy, green, and even yellow.

1
Put a plastic bowl filled with crumpled chicken wire in a basket and half-fill it with water.

2
Make a base of berried ivy, then add long stems of hazel and alder catkins and forsythia.

3
Thread some white Christmas roses through.

4
Finish with more berried ivy trailing over the edge of the basket.

BEAT THE WINTER

Here you can see how it is possible to make an arrangement with a totally different feel using the same ingredients as before—white Christmas roses and yellow forsythia. The frosted Perspex plastic vase draws attention to the stems of the flowers. The whole effect is slightly Japanese.

1
Choose a flat, narrow vase and three-quarters-fill it with water.

2
Cut all the forsythia to the same height and put it in the vase.

3
Weave some Christmas roses through the arrangement.

LEMON BASKET

This mouthwatering arrangement
of lemons, pittosporum, lady's
mantle, and gerberas makes me
think of a game of tennis on a sunny
summer afternoon. I'm longing for
a glass of homemade lemonade and
a slice of luscious lemon cake.
I can't think of anything more perfect.

The arrangement involves wired-up lemons and is simple to make, even if it doesn't look it. Gerberas play a big part in the show, too. I've used some dainty mini gerberas so as not to overwhelm things.

1
Make a collar of chicken-wire without moss (page 300) and wire it to a plastic bowl.

2
Push a length of wire through each lemon and twist the ends together.

3
Wire two rows of lemons to the collar. Fill the bowl with crumpled chicken wire, then add water.

4
Make a base of variegated pittosporum and lady's mantle, then add clusters of bright yellow and palest green mini gerberas.

LOOKING FOXY

It was when I was decorating a friend's house for a party that I noticed this spot on the landing. It needed a large and fairly classical arrangement, so I filled a great black cast-iron urn with a mass of late-summer flowers, including tall foxtail lilies. It shows the beautiful harmonies that can be created if you use the full range of yellows, from pale greenish yellow to a dark rusty orange.

I love the similarity of shape and form of these flowers. They are predominantly spiky but have different textures. The compact density of the millet grass reflects the cattails. The foxtail lilies are similar in shape, but have a looser, more airy habit.

1
Line an urn with plastic sheeting and fill with soaked florist's foam (page 300).

2
Use some green and yellow euonymus as a base, making sure that some of it trails over the edge of the urn.

3
Add a mass of tall foxtail lilies, allowing plenty of space between each flower head.

4
Add medium-length cattails and finish with plenty of millet grass around the base of the taller stems.

TIP:
If you pick off the lower flowers of the foxtail lilies as they fade, the stems can last two weeks or more.

EVERLASTING ROSES

A pair of creamware pots filled with dried yellow roses would suit a mantelpiece, dressing table, or attractive antique side table. They would also look classy—though totally different—on a glass-topped coffee table or on a pair of Perspex plastic side tables on either side of a bed.

1
Fill your pots with a round ball of florist's foam —the type for dried flowers— leaving a third of the foam above the rim.

2
Put rows of rose heads in place, starting around the rim of the pot.

3
Continue row by row until you reach the center of the pot.

ROWS OF ROSES

What a difference a container makes! The owner of this house was expecting a formal arrangement of roses, lilies, and foliage for the console table in the hall. Instead I chose the more audacious alternative of stripes of orange and yellow roses in a rope-handled rough wooden tray. It certainly adds a touch of the unexpected.

There's no getting away from it. This arrangement will be expensive. That means you will want these roses to last as long as possible, so give them a good long drink of water before you arrange them.

1
Carefully line a wooden tray with heavy plastic sheeting, and fill it with blocks of soaked florist's foam (page 300).

2
Remove the foliage from the roses and trim the stems short and at an angle.

3
Starting at one edge of the tray, arrange rose heads to make the first block of color.

4
Continue adding roses, alternating the blocks of color, until the tray is full.

SUNFLOWERS TO GO

I love old wooden crates for arranging flowers. They have so much character. The trick when using them is not to do anything too fussy. Let the crate speak for itself. Here I've simply planted it with sunflowers.

1
Line a crate with heavy plastic sheeting, and plant it with six mini sunflowers. That's it!

■ TIP:
Fill the crate with bunches of dried roses for a winter arrangement.

BUTTERFLY SHOWERS

These golden shower orchids always remind me of miniature yellow butterflies, so delicate yet so vibrant when the sun shines through them. Here I have surrounded them with my favorite honeycomb candles. The rich texture and color of the candles are highlighted by the copper wire wrapped around them. The wire adds extra support and is a nice design detail, while the clusters of three small candles make a lovely finishing touch.

When you have finished making this arrangement you can level off the potting mix, then top-dress with wheat, moss, or lichen. Don't overwater, and try to keep the arrangement out of strong sunlight.

1
Make a collar of chicken-wire without moss (page 300), and wire it to a plastic bowl.

2
Push a piece of wire through each candle, twist its ends together, and wire the candles to the collar upside down.

3
Wrap copper wire around the outside of the candles, and add groups of three small candles, using more wire.

4
Pot the orchids in the bowl, leaving the aerial roots showing. Support the orchids using natural canes and copper wire.

SPURGE

These beautiful green flowers add a touch of the vividly unexpected to an arrangement. To my mind the best variety is Euphorbia characias ssp. wulfenii, a perennial with bluish green leaves and nodding flowers. Euphorbia polychroma comes a close second.

■ If you want a spring hand-tied bouquet, nothing beats spurge combined with beautiful pale lemon yellow hyacinths.
■ Alternatively, try spurge as a collar around a few stems of acid green cymbidium orchids in a vase.

BEAR GRASS

Useful for its delicate, loose habit, this native of Texas and the Mexican highlands will add an exciting sense of movement to any arrangement.

■ Bear grass is very effective when simply worked into hand-tied bouquets.

■ Use just a few stems to lend a touch of softness to arrangements with a more graphic look.

MAGNOLIA GRANDIFLORA

This is a real garden favorite of mine, especially effective when it is grown against a wall. Its sturdy, shapely leaves have a wonderful suede-effect underside.

■ Try using it as a base foliage for a mixed arrangement with large flowers like peonies and hydrangeas.

■ You can also glue its flat leaves onto a container to cover it in preparation for holding a flower arrangement or a simple votive light.

ANTHURIUM

These very distinctive heart-shaped, dark green, glossy leaves last extremely well in water.

■ I love to use them to make a bold, defining collar around the edge of a vase.

■ A single leaf looks great with a stem of any striking flower—amaryllis is a good companion.

VIBURNUM OPULUS

This wonderful shrub is a "must" for any flower lover's garden and for every flower arranger. As its acid-green flowers grow, they develop into puffy, creamy white balls.

■ It makes a fabulous collar around long-stemmed white roses tied into a "tree" and placed in a vase lined with white pebbles.

■ Alternatively, try it with white lilac for a lovely, loose country feel.

HORSETAIL

This striking foliage has an interesting form and texture and has many uses. Try it to add height. It can even be bent into shape, and spray-painted.

■ Try gluing some cut stems of horsetail to the outside of a container to dress it up.

■ Submerge it in water in a clear glass vase so its fascinating stems are sharply magnified.

PAPYRUS

This amazing plant bears an enormous profusion of grasslike tufts from its lush green fibrous stem.

■ Added to any arrangement, papyrus foliage imparts a strong sense of structure.
■ Try it by itself with its tufts all trimmed to the same length.

SWISS CHEESE PLANT

The Swiss cheese plant has one of the most distinctive leaf forms I have ever used. Don't regard it as just some boring houseplant that gathers dust in a corner.

■ Try its glossy green, deeply cut leaves as an edging to an arrangement.
■ My favorite way of using it is under water in a clear glass vase to help disguise the stems of flowers.

GALAX

This useful plant from eastern North America has evergreen leaves, which often turn bronze in winter. They can last up to three weeks in water, so they are very useful for flower arranging.

■ They make a very pretty edging to a hand-tied bouquet.

■ Try them wrapped around glass votive lights, held in place with a narrow piece of raffia. These make a simple summer table decoration.

FAN PALM

Palm leaves are a must for any tropical arrangement, and they also make a fabulous edging for a tropical hand-tied bouquet.

■ Try them laid flat on the table as a base for a display of tropical fruit.

■ Spray some leaves gold, and use them to make an ever-so-unusual Christmas arrangement.

GARRYA ELLIPTICA

This is another great garden shrub. It is at its most beautiful in winter and early spring. The neutral color of its long, silky catkins makes it very versatile for flower arranging.

■ Try it in a hand-tied bouquet of roses arranged in a dome shape. Any color rose will look good.

■ Its amazing silver-green catkins add an air of mystery and a sense of movement to any arrangement.

FEATHERED PAPYRUS

This lush green foliage has a tropical-marsh quality.

■ Mix it with anthurium leaves, fan palm, and some clumps of horsetail to make an unusual arrangement of tropical foliage.

■ Cut a number of stems all to the same length, and tie them together into a ball shape. They will look like an oriental-style topiary.

ASPIDISTRA

This was once very popular as a tough houseplant, but I like to use it for its bold architectural foliage. It lasts very well in water.

- Fold some aspidistra leaves to make a dramatic edge to a hand-tied bouquet.
- You can also use them as a collar to frame a vase full of flowers, all of the same variety. Any flowers will look good with them.

MING FERN

The airy-looking foliage of the Ming fern has a strongly oriental character that suits the company of other oriental plants.

- Use it for a simple but stylish arrangement with a few stems of cymbidium or phalaenopsis orchids.
- Try an ikebana-style arrangement with some Viburnum opulus.

CYCAS PALM

This dramatic, glossy dark green
leaf has a very strong character that
only flowers of a similar strength
can stand up to.

■ Try combining it with some bold
white flowers like amaryllis, or
'Casablanca' lilies.
■ Want a sense of the tropics?
Line a vase with cycas palm leaves,
add soaked florist's foam and a mass
of tall gingers, all the same height.

Get the look
with greens

The color of grasses and foliage, green is so easy to take for granted. But broaden your mind. There's the fresh green of narcissus foliage, the acid green of spurge bracts, the soft green of Viburnum opulus. Green adds contrast to any arrangement—but you'll find it works just as well on its own.

FORMAL FOLIAGE

Constance Spry brought flower arranging into the English public eye after the gloomy war years. This shape of vase is very much associated with her. I filled it with an assortment of greenery—to show that a perfect display does not necessarily need to include any flowers. The varied textures of the different foliages evoke an old-fashioned sense of style that is best suited to a classic interior.

■ TIP:
The neutral
container allows
you to add some
clusters of red
flowers if you
wished.

The foliages here include Viburnum tinus, 'Gloire de Marengo' Canary Island ivy, smoke-tree foliage, two types of eucalyptus, Mexican orange, Rosa glauca syn. R. rubrifolia, Euonymus japonicus 'Aureus', and Brachyglottis 'Sunshine'.

1
Fill the vase with crumpled chicken wire and half-fill with water.

2
Make a base of Mexican orange brachyglottis, and euonymus Keep it compact and rounded.

3
Add contrast with clusters of smoke-tree foliage and height with long stems of Rosa glauca and eucalyptus.

4
Finally, weave in trailing stems of ivy and viburnum with its berries.

SUMMER CELEBRATION

This all-green arrangement of brachyglottis, lavender cotton, spiky variegated dracaena, variegated pittosporum, and long-leafed eucalyptus is another example of how foliage doesn't always need a floral accompaniment. The four church candles add height and could be lit for a nighttime party.

1
Use florist's tape to fix a ring of wet florist's foam (see page 300) to the rim of a glass bowl.

2
Push four church candles firmly into the foam ring.

3
Fill the ring with a mass of foliage, keeping the overall shape frothy. Make sure you disguise the edge of the ring.

■ TIP:
You don't need
a special glass
vase. A salad bowl
will do just as well.

ADD SOME FLOWERS

The arrangement takes on a different personality with flowers. You could use red for a Valentine's Day party or a ruby wedding anniversary, or blue and yellow for a summer party. Here I've added some beautifully scented white flowers—great for a wedding or christening.

1
After attaching the foam ring (page 190), use double-sided tape to fix three glass votive lights inside the bowl.

2
Add water to come halfway up the side of the votive lights.

3
Make the foliage base (page 190), then add white stocks and white sweet peas in clusters of three.

4
Add clusters of three or five—depending on the size of bowl—large-headed white 'Tineke' and 'Margaret Merril' roses.

TWO-TIER PAPYRUS

The inspiration for this minimalist arrangement of papyrus grass was the curvaceous vase, with its frosted-glass foot. The bowl of the vase magnifies the stems of the papyrus in a very beautiful manner. The finished result has an oriental feel to it.

1
Trim some papyrus so their heads peep out over the neck of the vase.

2
Trim their heads to a rounded shape, then add two more tall stems of papyrus and trim their heads flat.

3
Break up the formal lines with a few long spikes of horsetail.

4
Fill with water to the neck of the vase.

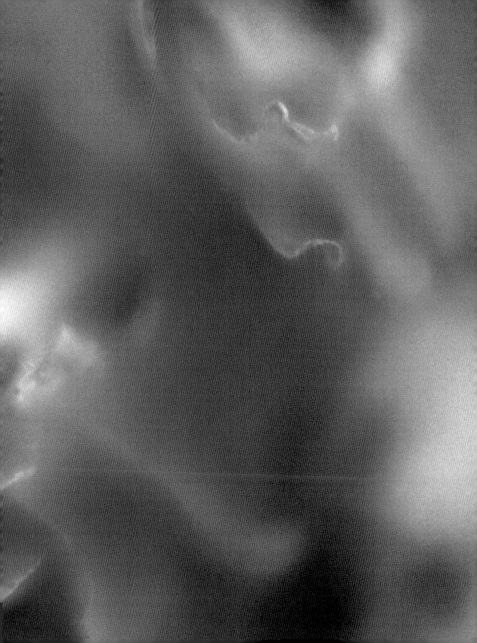

HYACINTH

Hyacinths are very versatile. You can pack lots of stems in a simple vase, or you can use the bulbs and enjoy watching them grow.

■ Deep blue hyacinths resonate alongside purple lisianthus, but add some white snapdragons or tulips to give a nautical effect.

■ Put a white hyacinth planted in a creamware pot at each guest's place at a wedding party, with a plant label for the guest's name. A lovely souvenir.

EUCALYPTUS

There are many varieties of this native of Australia, most of which are very useful in arrangements. Some are flowering, some have pointed leaves, and others have large round leaves.

■ Try short lengths of flowering eucalyptus in hand-tied bouquets or as a base for table decorations.

■ Longer stems of any eucalyptus will bowl you over in a tall urn.

DELPHINIUM

Blue delphiniums have such an intensity of color that they're hard to ignore, whether in a vase at home or in a border in the garden.

■ How about trying a fan of twelve long stems in a giant goldfish bowl lined with Indian grass? It will look sensational.

■ If you have delphiniums in the garden, remember that they grow tall and have very heavy flower heads, so they need staking.

GLOBE THISTLE

Glistening globe thistles have such a wonderful, graphic shape and rich, purple-blue color. Fresh or dried, I love them.

■ Use the dried heads to make topiary trees. As long as you keep them out of strong sunlight, they will keep their color well.

■ Try three saucers in a row on a low coffee table. Fill each with a ball of wet florist's foam studded with fresh globe thistle heads.

SILVER BIRCH

Silver birch always conjures up images of the vast Russian steppes, where the trees grow in profusion.

■ The twigs are beautiful just as they are for adding height to an arrangement. You could also try them to add spikiness to a dried-foliage hand-tied bouquet.

■ Spray some blue and pop a bunch in a tall galvanized pot.

ANEMONE

Yet another example of nature's wonderful way with blue. These are of a blue that almost verges on purple. Their petals are so richly dark that you can hardly see their soft black centers.

■ A nosegay of blue anemones would be a treat for a junior bridesmaid at a blue-and-white themed wedding.

■ Trim anemone stems down, and pack them tightly into a florist's foam ring for a table decoration.

EUCALYPTUS PODS

I love using eucalyptus pods, not only because of their fascinating shape and familiar aroma, but also because of their color—they look as if they have been frosted.

■ They make a festive hand-tied bouquet with Christmas foliage and wired-up dried oranges, nuts, and cinnamon sticks.

■ Want something scented? Then try eucalyptus pods in a hand-tied bouquet of white roses, white tulips, and blue spruce.

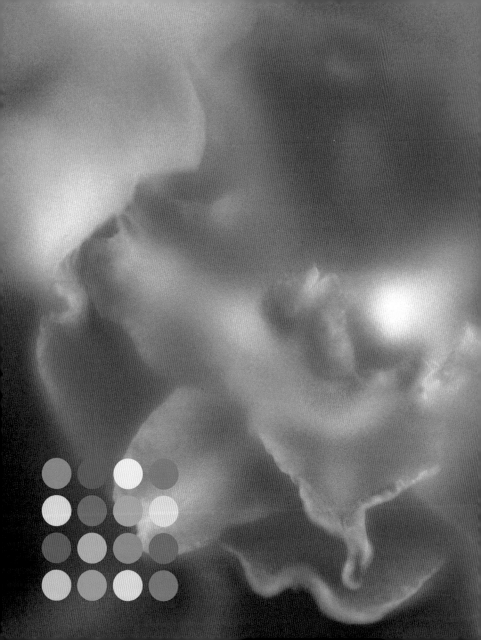

Get the look
with blues

Blue arrangements are so versatile. They can inject subtlety into a room or make you stop dead in your tracks. Think blue-gray eucalyptus or jewel-like deep blue anemones. Cool down blue arrangements with some white. Hot them up with orange. The choice is yours.

BLUE CURVES

Grape hyacinths are among my favorite spring bulbs. They look stunning massed together, and this vase is perfect for that kind of treatment. Its gentle curves echo the curves of the tiny flowers.

1
Arrange the grape hyacinths in your hand to give a shape that you like.

2
Trim the stems then pop them in the vase.

3
Loosen the stems a little.

4
Weave in a few of their leaves for contrast.

■ TIP:
Try some lily of
the valley in
a blue vase for a
similar effect,
but in reverse!

CORNFLOWER FROSTING

If you have an old wrought-iron balcony, this arrangement is just for you. Seeing the stems of the cornflowers through the frosted glass reminds me of hazy summer skies. If you haven't got a balcony, then just use one vase on a wrought-iron table.

1
Line up three frosted-glass vases along the balcony, and fill them all with water to the same level.

2
Arrange some cornflowers loosely in your hand.

3
Trim the stems and put a bunch in each vase.

DELPHINIUMS TO DIE FOR

In general, garden-grown delphiniums
shed their petals indoors sooner
than the commercially cultivated ones,
but I find that the dark blue 'Blue
Bees', the cream 'Casablanca',
and the white Pacific Giant hybrids
that I have used here all last well.
Putting the shades together like this
makes them look rather unreal.
Some of the colors have a luster
to them which gives them an almost
crystalline translucency.

Delphiniums are classic flowers for classic arrangements. Sometimes I use very long-stemmed delphiniums to add stateliness to a mixed, cottage-garden arrangement, but here you can see that they manage perfectly well by themselves.

1
Use a tall, rectangular, clear glass vase to contrast with the soft, heavy heads of the delphiniums.

2
Fill it three-quarters full with water.

3
Use the best blooms as the tall specimens. Cut them all to the same length and stand them in the vase.

4
Support them with a few more shorter stems arranged at the front.

■ TIP:
You can achieve
the same effect
if you use purple
African violet
plants instead.

VIOLET UPDATE

Violets, with their vibrant depth of color and heady scent, are wonderfully old-fashioned. Here I've given them a modern treatment, with painted pots in a geometric layout. Violets have short stems and a tendency to wilt quickly, so enjoy this arrangement while you can.

1
Paint nine matching terra-cotta pots with lilac paint, and paint nine saucers silver.

2
Put a glass liner in each pot, then add water.

3
Arrange three bunches of violets, edged with their leaves, in each pot.

4
Set the pots out in three rows of three.

TOWERING HYACINTHS

Sponge-like gray lichen and conical glass vases that fit into a metal tower make unusual use of tall blue hyacinths—one of the most common spring-flowering bulbs. If you don't have a tower-like planter, such as the one I've used, you could simply plant the hyacinths in the same way but in a deep glass dish. It would look stunningly cosmopolitan sitting on a glass coffee or dining table.

My blue hyacinth tower was perfect for this modern sunroom. The fact that the hyacinths are growing softens the whole effect. I love the reflection of it all in the mirror and couldn't wait to get the finished tower into position.

1
Support each conical glass vase in a deep container.

2
Put some gravel in the bottom of each vase, then fill them with gray lichen.

3
Plant an odd number of blue hyacinths in the vases, adding plenty of potting mix around their roots.

4
Water well, top with more lichen, then put the vases in the planter.

■ TIP:
You don't need
any water. The
lavender will
slowly dry and
gently fade.

LAVENDER'S BLUE

Lavender is usually associated with traditional country interiors. A mass of it stuffed in an old terracotta pot looks as if it has just come from the garden. That same concept, but approached in a contemporary way, can work in a modern setting.

1
Choose three square matching galvanized metal pots.

2
Cram them full of lavender all cut to the same length.

3
Trim the lavender carefully for a perfectly flat tabletop effect. This works really well with the straight-sided pots.

BLUE MOON

Christmas is a time of year when people like to decorate their front door with a wreath to welcome their guests. Here I have taken the traditional Christmas wreath but have given it a new slant by using shades of blue instead of the usual green, red, and gold. This wreath offers a scented bonus—eucalyptus and lavender, as well as the resinous scent of the blue spruce.

The gourd wreath is not as difficult to make as it looks, and when it is finished it should last around four weeks—so it is well worth the bother. Your visitors will thank you for it.

1
Start with a moss collar (page 300) made into a circle.

2
Wire up sprigs of blue spruce, then wire them into the circle, their tips all going in the same direction.

3
Add crisscross clusters of lavender, their stems all cut to the same length and tied with raffia.

4
Finally, wire in groups of three gourds and clusters of eucalyptus pods.

SYMPHONY IN BLUE

I often remember seeing huge vases with an array of different-colored gladioluses on my mother's sideboard. Times have changed. Many people now prefer them all the same color and are happy to glory in the beauty of their individual flowers.

1
Line three terracotta flowerpots with plastic sheeting and fill with soaked florist's foam (page 300).

2
Carefully remove lilac-blue gladiolus heads—with a nice fat bud if possible—from their stems.

3
Place heads and buds in each of the pots, and line up in a row.

THE AUDACITY OF IT!

Look what you get when you opt for an audacious combination of color and shape! This classic arrangement goes stratospheric when zingy orange meets deep, rich purple. The whole effect is lifted another notch or two by the translucent blue glass vase.

1
Fill a tall, fairly narrow clear blue vase with a base of fine-leafed flowering eucalyptus and round-leafed brachyglottis.

2
Add sea holly, with its jagged, silvery bracts, followed by "punctuation marks" of purple, cup-shaped lisianthus. Aim for a rounded shape.

3
Weave in some orange 'Pareo' roses and finally some stems of eucalyptus to disguise the edge of the vase.

FLOWERING CHERRY

These flowers always remind me of spring. Long before the leaves emerge, their blossom is the first sign of life after winter.

■ Simply try a mass of stems in a clear glass vase with just a little water.

■ Weave some of the supple stems through a wicker basket, and plant with 'Paper White' narcissi for a charming springtime table arrangement.

PHALAENOPSIS ORCHID

The arching stems of the much-loved moth orchid look best just on their own. It also comes in hot pink and cream.

■ For a contemporary, long-lasting arrangement, show off the roots. Carefully wash the soil off, and put the whole plant in a tall clear glass vase with a few inches of water.

■ If you have only a few stems, try submerging them completely in a large glass vase of water.

DENDROBIUM ORCHID

The white dendrobium orchid is my favorite. Other stunners are the striking purple 'Madame de Pompadour' and the dark orange-red 'James Storey', often used with autumn foliage and evergreens.

■ Pop a pot of white dendrobium in a clear, lime green, pebble-lined container for a zingy combination.

■ If you want a more traditional look, plant one in a rustic container and "fence" it in with some twigs.

GLADIOLUS

Fashionable about thirty years ago, the gladiolus is due, I think, for a revival.

■ Find the tallest clear glass vase you can—tall enough for a complete stem—and add a mass of them with just 2 inches of water.

■ Try them in a vase lined with aspidistra leaves and with a folded aspidistra-leaf collar. Add a "frame" of shrubby dogwood, and tie the flower stems to it with fine white cord.

BELLS OF IRELAND

A lovely annual that, in the garden, grows multi-stemmed, rather than with the single, slender stems it has when grown commercially. The tiny, tubular white flowers hide coyly away in their shell-like calyx.

■ These look great in a hand-tied bouquet, where they add graceful height and structure.

■ Use them tall in a vase lined with green pebbles and with a collar of cream or white gerberas.

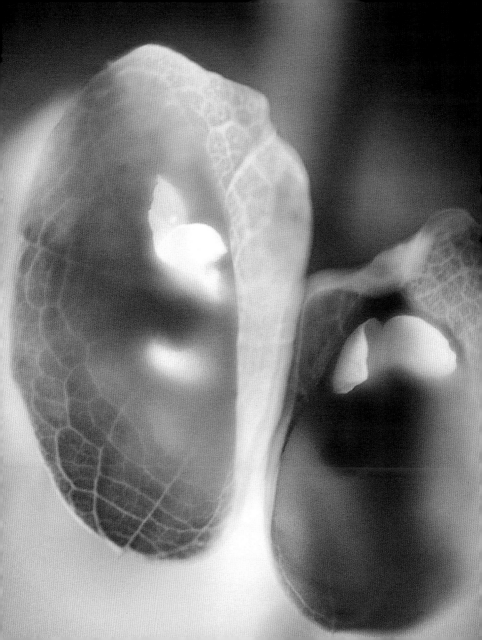

TUBEROSE

Originally from Mexico, tuberoses have a heavy, rich, romantic scent and the most amazing creamy white flowers, often tinged with pink.

■ Traditional meets modern when you fan them out in a conical vase with some Indian grass fed through to fill the gaps.
■ Alternatively use them fairly short in a dome-shaped bouquet, sitting in a clear vase lined with slices of lime.

AMARYLLIS

This is a stately, architectural bulb, which is easy to grow yourself to brighten up the home in winter.

■ For Christmastime, try planting three or five red amaryllis in a dark wooden bowl or basket.

■ White amaryllis look good in galvanized or creamware pots, topped with gray lichen.

JASMINE

When you look at this jasmine, with
its beautiful pink-tinged petals,
you can almost smell its wonderful,
heady fragrance.

■ Put a jasmine plant in a
creamware pot, and support it with
twigs of silver birch.
■ For a contemporary location,
simply spray its dried, twining stems
with silver paint and pop them at an
angle in the narrow neck of a vase.

TULIP

Tulips come in pure white as well as white flecked with pink or green—and sometimes both.

■ Gently bend some long white tulips and put the whole lot—stems and all—in a large goldfish bowl with just a small amount of water colored green with food dye.

■ White tulips look great with white phalaenopsis orchids in a hand-tied bouquet with variegated foliage.

BRACHYGLOTTIS 'SUNSHINE'

This silvery gray evergreen has got to be one of my all-time favorite foliages, both in the garden and for flower arranging. It will add an English country feel to anything you care to mix it with.

■ Try it with baby-pink peonies or roses in a vase or hand-tied bouquet.
■ Brachyglottis looks especially good in all-white compositions, where it adds a slightly wintry look.

ANTHURIUM

These exotic-looking flowers last
a few days without water, but give
them a good long drink first.

■ Put a wet block of florist's foam in
an opaque vase so it stands a yard
higher than the vase, make a chicken-wire frame around the foam, and
cover it with heads of white
anthuriums—a real talking point.

■ Beautiful in other colors, too; try
a hand-tied bouquet of mixed
chocolate brown, red, and orange.

NERINE

This flower originally came from
South Africa. It ranges from
pale pink and white to hot pinks,
reds, lilacs, and purples.

■ Arrange the stems in a grid
pattern in a cube-shaped vase, then
add some short eucalyptus foliage
to fill it out, yet keep it airy.

■ Alternatively, bind the stems in
a couple of places with green
metallic wire to make a "tree," and
arrange at an angle in a glass tank.

Get the look with whites

You can't go wrong with white. There are whites to go with everything—crisp and clear, creamy, or green-tinged. An all-white arrangement looks coolly classic, but put white in an arrangement of other colors, and you'll lighten it up right away.

TIP:
Lilac does not last very well, so cut its stems at an angle to improve its chances.

LILAC TIME

You must take care that the container you choose doesn't overwhelm white flowers. This metallic vase, narrow at the base and wider at the top, was perfect for the natural loose look I wanted to achieve with my beautiful bunch of white lilac.

1
Half-fill a vase with water, and trim some lilac so it is about twice as tall as the vase.

2
Arrange the lilac loosely in the vase.

3
Finish with some short sprigs of eucalyptus leaves to soften the edge of the vase.

NERINE SNAKE

This arrangement uses one of my favorite, most versatile vases.
I call it the snake vase. You can see it also on page 120, where I have made it into a circle.

1
Fill each tube of the vase with water roughly halfway, and cut the nerines all to the same length.

2
Tuck a single galax leaf around the stems of some of the nerines. Pop them in most of the tubes.

3
Cut some pieces of variegated papyrus all to the same length, fold, and tie into loops using lengths of raffia.

4
Put the folded papyrus into the remaining test tubes.

DRIFTWOOD AND ORCHIDS

Orchids bring a touch of exoticism to any room. Here I have planted them in a deep glass bowl, which I have lined with pebbles and lichen. The piece of driftwood and fine bamboo canes give the whole arrangement a slightly oriental flavor.

1
Arrange gray pebbles and gray lichen around the edges of a deep glass bowl.

2
Plant three moth orchids in the center, using special orchid potting mix, and water well.

3
Tie each orchid stem to a fine bamboo cane, using raffia. Add some purely decorative raffia ties as well.

4
Top the soil with more lichen, and end by putting a piece of drift-wood in the arrangement.

HEAVEN SENT

What could be simpler or more elegant and opulent than this mass of lovely pinkish white, heavenly scented 'Heritage' garden roses in a cut-glass vase? They look as if they've just been picked.

1
Choose a low, wide-necked vase and half-fill with water.

2
Put the shorter roses around the neck of the vase.

3
Use a mixture of open blooms and half-open buds, some with their leaves.

4
Build up the height with long-stemmed roses, keeping the arrangement looking natural.

STRAWBERRIES AND CREAM

Pink 'Doris Ryker' spray roses look lovely on their own, but they are much more eye-catching with some large, round, creamy-white garden roses for contrast. This combination of roses would make a lovely hand-tied bouquet, too.

1
Half-fill a tall glass vase with water.

2
Arrange the 'Doris Ryker' roses in your hand into a tall, fan-shaped, loose bouquet.

3
Trim their stems to one length, and put them in the vase.

4
Weave through some creamy white garden roses to punctuate the arrangement.

HAT TRICK

At the height of summer, what could be more delightful than to wear a hat decorated with blowsy, scented old garden roses? This one uses a mass of roses in a variety of sizes and colors, some in full bloom, others half open.

1
Bend a medium florist's wire two-thirds of the way along.

2
Wrap its long end around a rose stem and around its own short end.

3
Wind spool wire around the wire of the first rose, and join it to the next.

4
Complete the rose garland, arrange it on the hat, and fasten its ends with wire.

■ TIP:
Keep the hat cool
and out of direct
sunlight until you
are ready to wear it.

ICED MAGIC

White 'Margaret Merril' roses and green 'Viridiflora' spray roses are so special that they do not need any accompaniment. I hope that the simple treatment I have given them here conveys the idea of a traditional English rose garden at the height of summer.

1
Choose a rectangular frosted glass vase to set off the roses. Half-fill with water.

2
Make a base of green spray roses, arranging them into a broad fan shape. Weave in plenty of the 'Margaret Merril' roses.

3
Position a few more white roses so they over-hang the edge of the vase.

BELLE OF THE BALL

Cultivated white bluebells have a
stateliness that their blue country
cousins lack. Here a modern frosted
Perspex plastic vase magnifies their
bright green fleshy stems and softens
the effect of the green–white contrast.

1
Choose a flat
rectangular
vase and
three-quarters-
fill it with water.

2
Trim the stems
of the bluebells
all to the
same length.

3
Place them in
the vase,
ensuring that
they are
not bunched up
too tightly.

■ TIP:
Remember that
the finished
mirror frame will
be a lot larger
than at the start.

FLOWER-GARLAND MIRROR

Grinling Gibbons was the master of English woodcarving and is the inspiration behind this design for a Victorian bedroom mirror. I hope it looks a little like the carved-wood mirror and picture frames made by him.

1
Staple chicken wire to the front of the mirror frame, and use it to make a dried-moss collar (page 300).

2
Trim wheat stems all to the same length, and wire them to the moss collar in evenly spaced criss-cross clusters.

3
Wire bunches of dried single and double fever-few and white everlasting, and add them to the collar, evenly spaced.

4
Add clusters of dried poppy heads, dried white peonies, and white roses, and finish with some wood-shaving "roses."

AGAPANTHUS AND FRIENDS

Busy-looking agapanthus needs to be balanced by something with strong, graphic lines. The leaves of the Swiss cheese plant fit the bill perfectly. Agapanthus and Swiss cheese both come in larger and smaller varieties. Here I have used the smaller 'Bressingham White' agapanthus.

1
Choose a fairly tall cylindrical glass vase and three-quarters-fill it with water.

2
Cut the stems of the agapanthus so their flowers stand well above the vase.

3
Finish with a couple of Swiss cheese leaves in the neck of the vase to form a wide collar.

SUBTLE HARMONY

This arrangement of tuberoses and Magnolia grandiflora leaves is nothing if not subtle. The texture and color of the underside of the magnolia leaves work so well with the nuts, while the spiky architectural tuberose flower heads echo the shape of the leaves.

1
Stand a plastic bowl in the center of a glass bowl, fixing it with florist's tape, then add water.

2
Put crumpled chicken wire in the bowl, then fill the space between bowl and glass with walnuts and chestnuts.

3
Make a base of magnolia leaves in the chicken wire.

4
Add single stems of tuberoses, evenly spaced through the foliage.

TIP:
The arrangement
is heavy, so
make sure the
plastic bowl
is well secured.

EUCHARIS BEAUTY

Eucharis is another white flower with a stunning scent, and for me that's always a bonus. It also lasts well as a cut flower. Here a few stems look magnificent with a "necklace" of flowering variegated 'Gloire de Marengo' Canary Island ivy.

1
Choose a tall vase with a heavy base and add water.

2
Arrange some lengths of flowering ivy around the neck of the vase to form a "necklace."

3
Add very long stems of eucharis—the tallest can be three times as tall as the vase.

4
Arrange them loosely and well-spaced among the ivy.

HOW TO MAKE A MOSS COLLAR

Fold chicken wire around a length of moss, and attach it to a bowl or basket using pieces of wire. Attach wired-up clusters of foliage or flowers to the collar to cover it.

FLORIST'S FOAM

Cut green florist's foam to shape, and place it in a bowl of water until it sinks to the bottom and air bubbles stop rising. Leave it to stand to allow excess water to drain out before using. Brown florist's foam is for dried flowers and should never be soaked.

With special thanks

to Sabrina Bemath for all her
kind help and useful advice.